Table of Contents

Chapter 1 : A New Beginning

Captain Jack, a brave and daring pirate, had just set sail on his ship, The Black Pearl, with a new crew. He was on a mission to find treasure and become the most feared pirate in the seven seas.

The crew could feel the excitement building as they sailed toward the horizon. They knew that with Captain Jack leading the way, anything was possible.

Chapter 2 : The Island of the Dead

As they sailed further into the sea, Captain Jack received a tip about a hidden treasure on the Island of the Dead. The island was known to be cursed, and no one had ever returned from there alive. However, Captain Jack had a burning desire to find the treasure and add it to his collection.

Chapter 3 : The Battle at Sea

As they approached the island, a rival pirate ship ambushed them. It was a fierce battle, and the crew fought bravely under Captain Jack's leadership. The Black Pearl emerged victorious, and the rival pirates fled. However, their victory was short-lived as they realized that their ship had been damaged in the battle.

<u>Chapter 4 : The Quest for Repairs</u>

Captain Jack knew that they needed to get the ship repaired if they were to continue their journey. They sailed to a nearby port and met a group of skilled shipwrights who agreed to repair the ship. However, they demanded a hefty sum of gold in return. Captain Jack had no choice but to agree to their terms and set sail once again with a repaired ship.

Chapter 5 : The Siren's Call

On their journey, they heard a beautiful voice calling out to them from the sea. It was the voice of a siren, and the crew was enchanted by it.

Captain Jack knew the dangers of the siren's call and ordered his crew to stay away. However, one of his crew members disobeyed his orders and jumped into the sea, lured by the siren's song.

Chapter 6 : The Underwater Kingdom

The crew member who had jumped into the sea was nowhere to be found, and Captain Jack knew that they had to find him before it was too late. They searched the sea and came across an underwater kingdom. The kingdom was ruled by a mermaid queen who had captured the crew member. Captain Jack had to negotiate with the queen to get his crew member back.

Chapter 7 : The Curse of the Aztec Gold

As they continued their journey, they stumbled upon a cursed treasure. It was the Aztec gold, and whoever possessed it would be cursed for eternity.

Captain Jack knew the dangers of the curse and decided to leave the treasure behind. However, one of his crew members was tempted by the wealth and took the gold for himself.

Chapter 8 : The Return of the Kraken

The crew member who had taken the Aztec gold was cursed, and the curse brought back an old enemy - the Kraken.

The Kraken was a giant sea monster that had attacked their ship before, and Captain Jack knew that they were in grave danger. They had to find a way to break the curse and defeat the Kraken before it was too late.

Chapter 9 : The Curse Broken

Captain Jack and his crew discovered that the only way to break the curse was to return the Aztec gold to its original resting place.

They sailed to the island where the gold was found and returned it to its rightful place. The curse was lifted, and the Kraken disappeared back into the depths of the sea.

Chapter 10 : The Mutiny

One of Captain Jack's crew members was unhappy with the leadership of Captain Jack and decided to start a mutiny. He convinced several other crew members to join him and took control of the ship. Captain Jack was left stranded on a deserted island, but he refused to give up. He had to find a way to get his ship back and defeat the mutineers.

<u>Chapter 11 : The Rescue</u>

Captain Jack managed to signal for help, and a friendly ship came to his rescue. He convinced the captain of the ship to help him get his ship back from the mutineers.

They sailed back to The Black Pearl and engaged in a fierce battle with the mutineers. Captain Jack emerged victorious, and the mutineers were forced to walk the plank.

Chapter 12 : The Final Showdown

Captain Jack had achieved his dream of becoming the most feared pirate in the seven seas, but he still had one enemy left to defeat - his rival pirate, Blackbeard. Blackbeard was known for his ruthless tactics and his desire to take over The Black Pearl. Captain Jack knew that this would be his toughest battle yet, but he was ready to face his enemy and defend his ship.

Epilogue

Captain Jack emerged victorious in his battle against Blackbeard, and he continued his adventures as a pirate. He went on to discover new lands, find more treasure, and become a legend in the pirate world.

The Adventures of a Brave Pirate had come to an end, but Captain Jack's legacy lived on forever.